FLOWERING VS. NON-FLOWERING PLANTS

KNOWING THE DIFFERENCE

Biology 3rd Grade | Children's Biology Books

BABY PROFESSOR
EDUCATION KIDS

Speedy Publishing LLC

40 E. Main St. #1156

Newark, DE 19711

www.speedypublishing.com

Copyright 2017

All Rights reserved. No part of this book may be reproduced or used in any way or form or by any means whether electronic or mechanical, this means that you cannot record or photocopy any material ideas or tips that are provided in this book

In this book, we're going to cover the difference between flowering and non-flowering plants. So, let's get right to it!

Lantana Plant

FLOWERING PLANTS VERSUS NON-FLOWERING PLANTS

Flowering plants have both female and male parts. These two parts are enclosed within their petals. They use the female and male parts of their flowers to reproduce.

Since they don't have flowers, non-flowering plants have other ways to reproduce and make sure their species continues. Non-flowering plants have been in existence on Earth much longer than flowering parts. Flowering plants are newcomers on the Earth compared to non-flowering plants.

Crown Fern

Corpse Lily
(Autotrophic Plant)

Most types of plants are autotrophic, which simply means they are able to produce their own food. Some types of plants are heterotrophic, which means they are parasites and must live on a host.

Plants are so diverse that they are classified into many different groups depending on their size, vascular bundles, and habitat, and whether they produce spores or seeds. The two major categories of classification are flowering and non-flowering. Both non-flowering and flowering plants are thought to have come from a common ancestor. Non-flowering land plants evolved about 475 million years ago. Flowering plants began in the Lower Cretaceous period, which was only about 130 million years ago.

Conifer

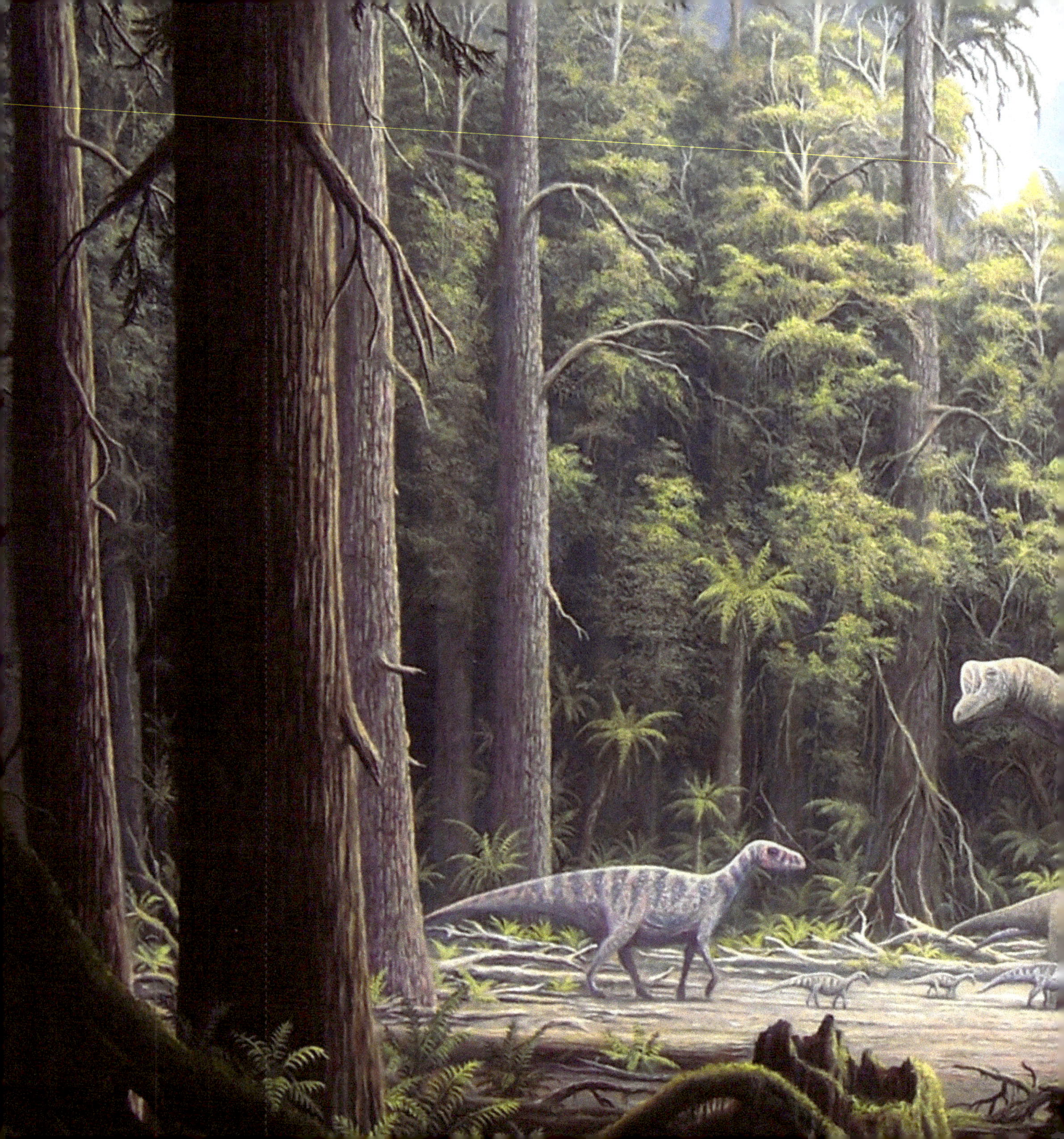

So flowering plants haven't been around as long as non-flowering plants. It's hard to believe that there was a time on Earth when there were no flowers at all, because flowers are everywhere today. The early Earth had towering trees and lots of ferns, but no flowers.

WHAT ARE FLOWERING PLANTS?

Flowering plants are vascular plants that grow flowers. Vascular simply means that they have tissues that carry water and minerals throughout the plant. The sole function of their flowers is reproduction. The flowers of the plant produce both male and female reproductive cells, pollen and eggs respectively.

Tulip Farm

Apple Flowers

Once pollinated and fertilized, they then produce seeds, which are the beginnings of the next-generation of plants. The seeds of flowering plants are surrounded by a fleshy or dry tissue that is called the fruit. Some of these fruits are fruits that people can eat. An apple tree is a flowering plant. It produces apple blossoms, which are flowers, and then it produces the apples, which are the fruit containing the seeds of the new apple trees.

Plants that have flowers after they mature are called angiosperms. The seeds of angiosperms have protective coats. Flowering plants are categorized into two main groups, monocots and dicots. Monocots have seeds that just have one embryonic leaf while dicots have two such leaves.

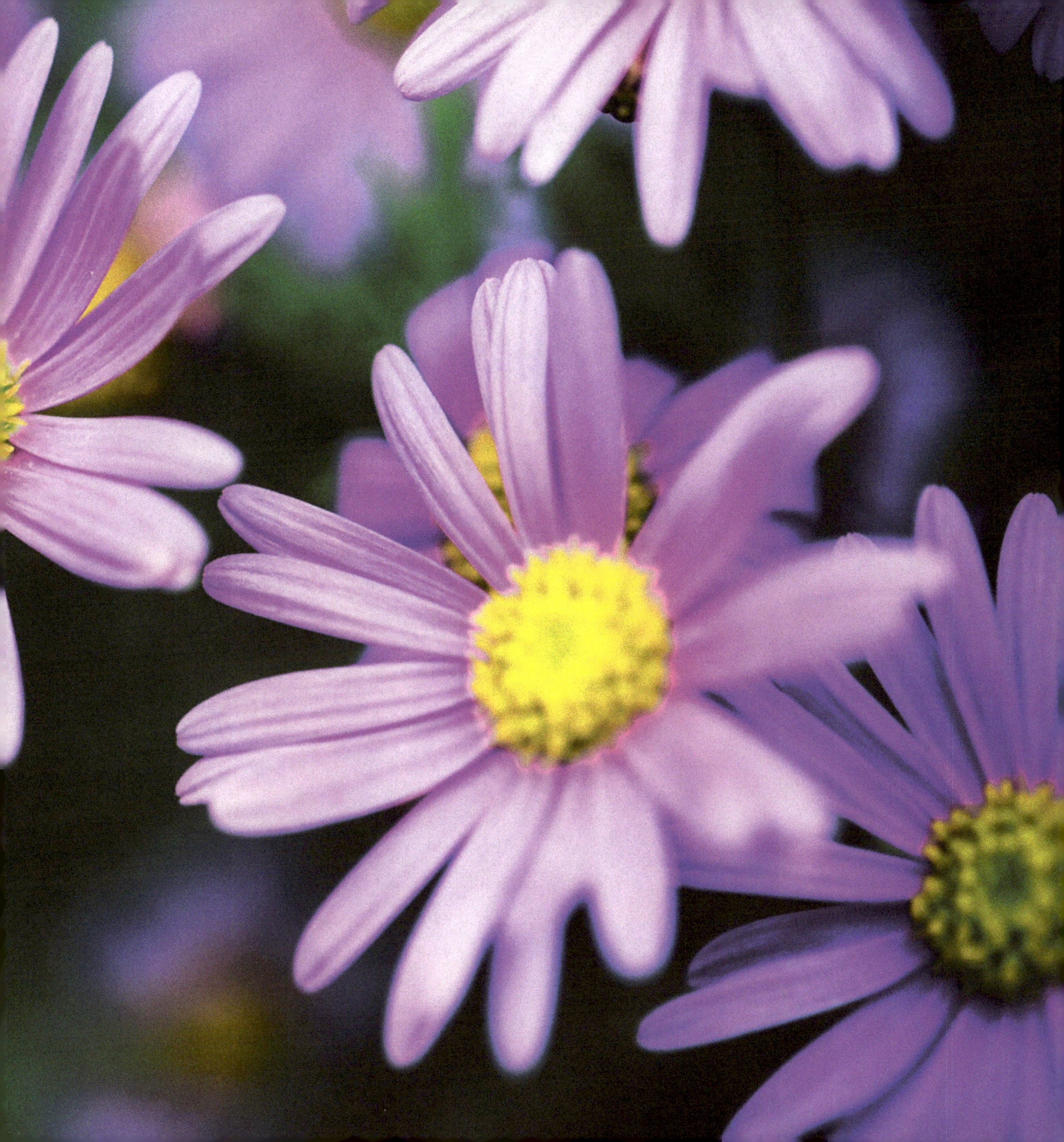

Rainforest

The flowers of a flowering plant give shelter to both the male and female reproductive parts. They also attract insects and birds that help the pollination process.

WHAT ARE NON-FLOWERING PLANTS?

Although non-flowering plants don't produce blooms, it doesn't mean they don't reproduce. They just have different ways of reproducing than flowering plants do. They have reproductive structures, such as spores and strobili, which are structures containing spores.

Life Cycle of a Fern

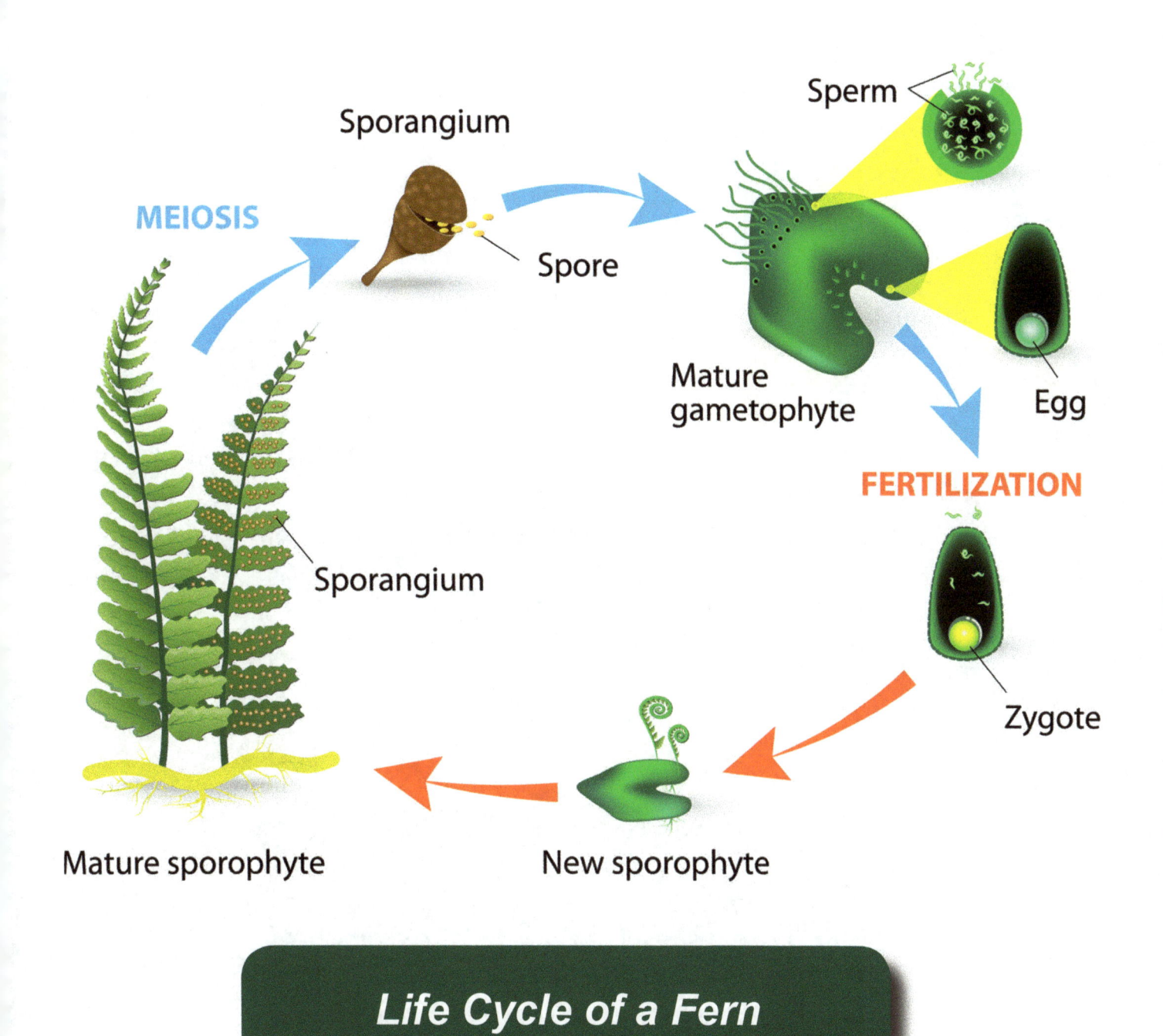

Mousse Bryophytes

THERE ARE THREE TYPES OF NON-FLOWERING PLANTS:

Bryophytes, which are simple plants that are nonvascular

Pteridophytes, which produce spores

Gymnosperms, which have seeds without a protective coat, the word gymnosperm means "naked seeds"

Mosses are examples of bryophytes. Ferns are examples of pteridophytes. Pteridophytes produce hundreds of spores. **Giant sequoia trees** are examples of gymnosperms.

Giant Sequoia

Young Cones

Conifers are one of the major groups of gymnosperms. They use cones for their seeds. They're woody plants. Some examples of conifers are redwood trees and fir trees. Some of a conifer's cones are male and some are female. The male cone produces pollen that is carried by the wind.

If the male pollen falls on a female cone, then that cone will be fertilized and produce seeds. If you've ever picked up a pinecone from the ground, you'll notice that they are hard and some have barbs. This structure protects the new seeds as they grow. When the seeds are ready, they're released by the cone. The conifer seeds actually are winged so they will float in the air to a new location!

Pine Cone

Vine on Bark

THE DIFFERENCE BETWEEN FLOWERING PLANTS AND NON-FLOWERING PLANTS

Suppose you go outdoors and you see a vine growing up a trellis. Is that vine a flowering or a non-flowering plant? You might think it's a non-flowering plant, since, when you observe it, it doesn't have any flowers on it. However, many flowering plants don't have blooms all the time. You'll have to find out if this vine has flowers at any time of the year.

If a plant already has flowers, it's easy to classify because you can see the blooms. Flowering plants have a multitude of different brightly colored flowers of all different shapes and sizes. In addition to this obvious way to tell the two different types of plants apart, there are other ways to classify them as well.

Vine with Purple Flowers

Colorful Flowers in Bloom

BIODIVERSITY

Even though flowering plants have been on the Earth for much less time than non-flowering plants, they now represent about 90% of the plant species on Earth. This means they have much more biodiversity than non-flowering plants. Orchids, roses, and daffodils are all flowering plants. Scientists estimate that there over 400,000 species of flowering plants. Samples of non-flowering plants are ferns, cycads, mosses, and pine.

COLOR

All plants that have chlorophyll to produce their own food have some green color, but the beautiful blues, pinks, yellows, and reds that we see in plants are almost exclusively in flowers. These colors help attract the insects and birds needed to help in pollination. Most non-flowering plants don't have a need to attract these organisms so instead they put their energy into catkins and cones, which are their structures for dispersing pollen.

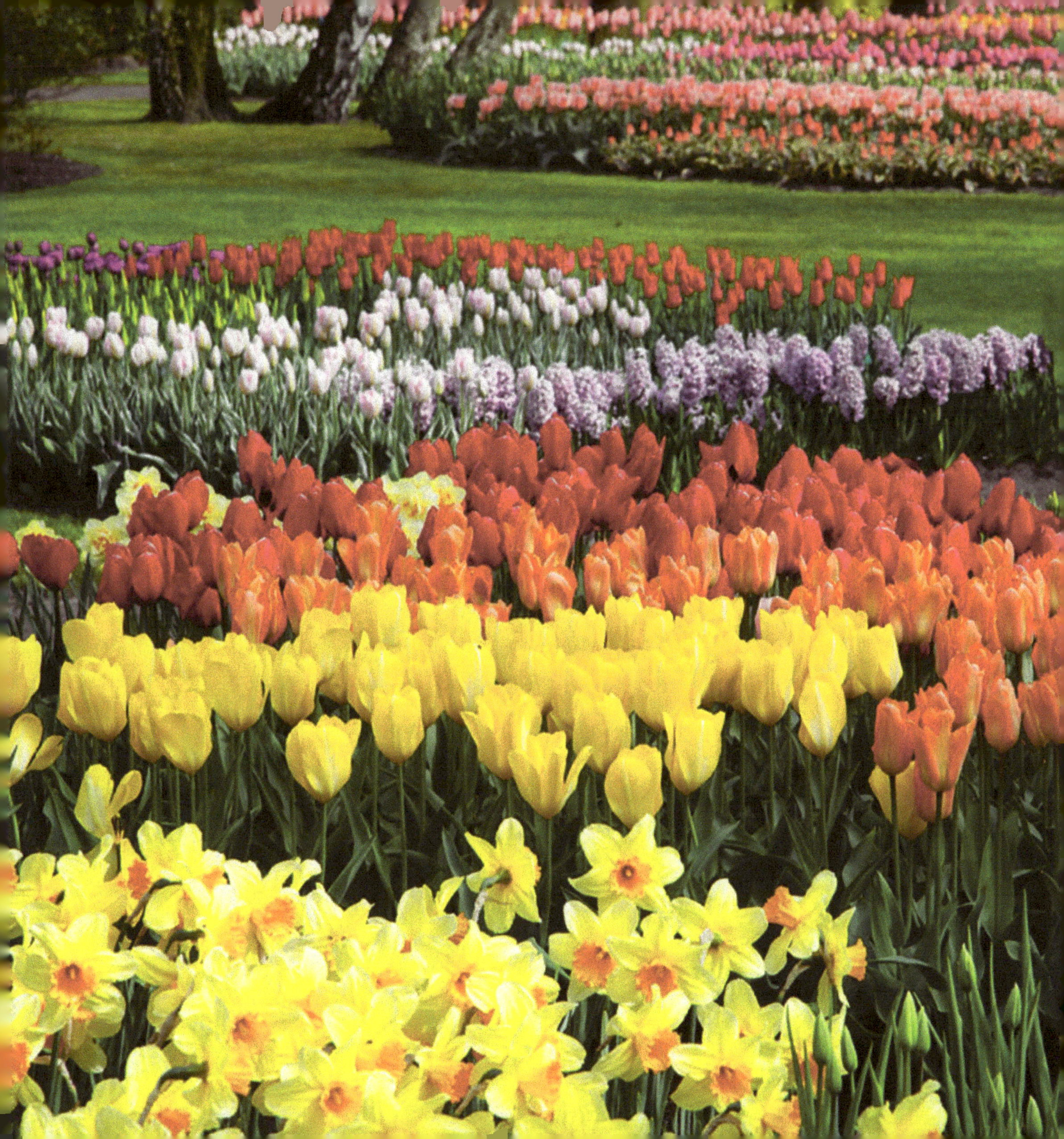

Butterfly on Top a Flower

ATTRACTING ANIMALS

Animals and insects eat both types of plants, so both types of plants are susceptible to pests. However, flowering plants have more complex relationships with animals and insects since they also attract birds, bees, and butterflies to consume their nectar and pollen without harming the plant.

In return for this food, these creatures help pollinate the plants. They aren't performing this service to the plant on purpose, they are just there to eat the nectar. It's accidental that the pollen gets stuck to them and then is transferred to the female part of the plant.

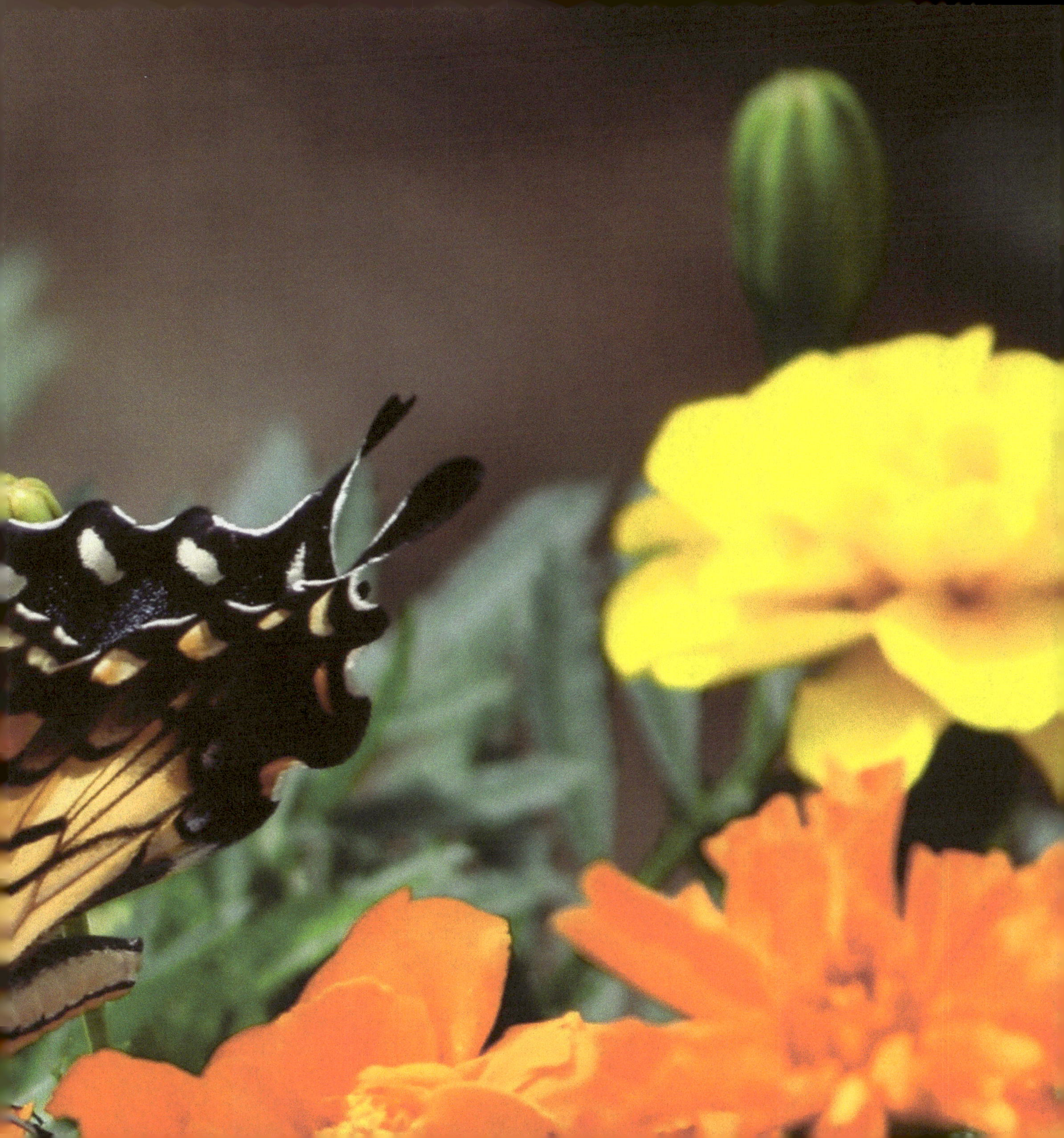

Red Moss

VASCULAR SYSTEM

All plants that fall in the category of flowering have a well-developed vascular system. This means they have xylem and phloem for absorbing and moving nutrients and water throughout the plant.

Some non-flowering plants don't have this structure. Some mosses, for example, live in aquatic or other very moist areas since they don't have the ability to take in water and distribute it.

Flowering plants can more easily adapt to different environments than the simpler types of non-flowering plants.

Growing Plant

MODE OF PROPAGATION

The way they reproduce is one of the major differences between flowering and non-flowering plants. Non-flowering plants reproduce via spores and cones instead of through the use of flowers. However, some plants in each group can also reproduce through cuttings of roots, stems, and leaves.

This type of reproduction is called **asexual propagation**. For example, if you've ever started a new plant from cuttings from another plant, then you know how this type of reproduction works.

Asexual Propagation

Pollination

REPRODUCTIVE PROCESS

The beautiful, fragrant flowers from flowering plants help to attract birds and insects to help carry their male pollen cells from the stamen to the female part of the plant called the pistil. This process is called **pollination** and flowering plants need help from birds, insects, and the wind to move pollen to the female part of the plant so that fertilization can take place.

There are a few non-flowering plants that need this kind of help from other organisms too. Some non-flowering plants have cones that attract insects. However, most non-flowering plants reproduce on their own and produce plants that are genetically similar.

Fern

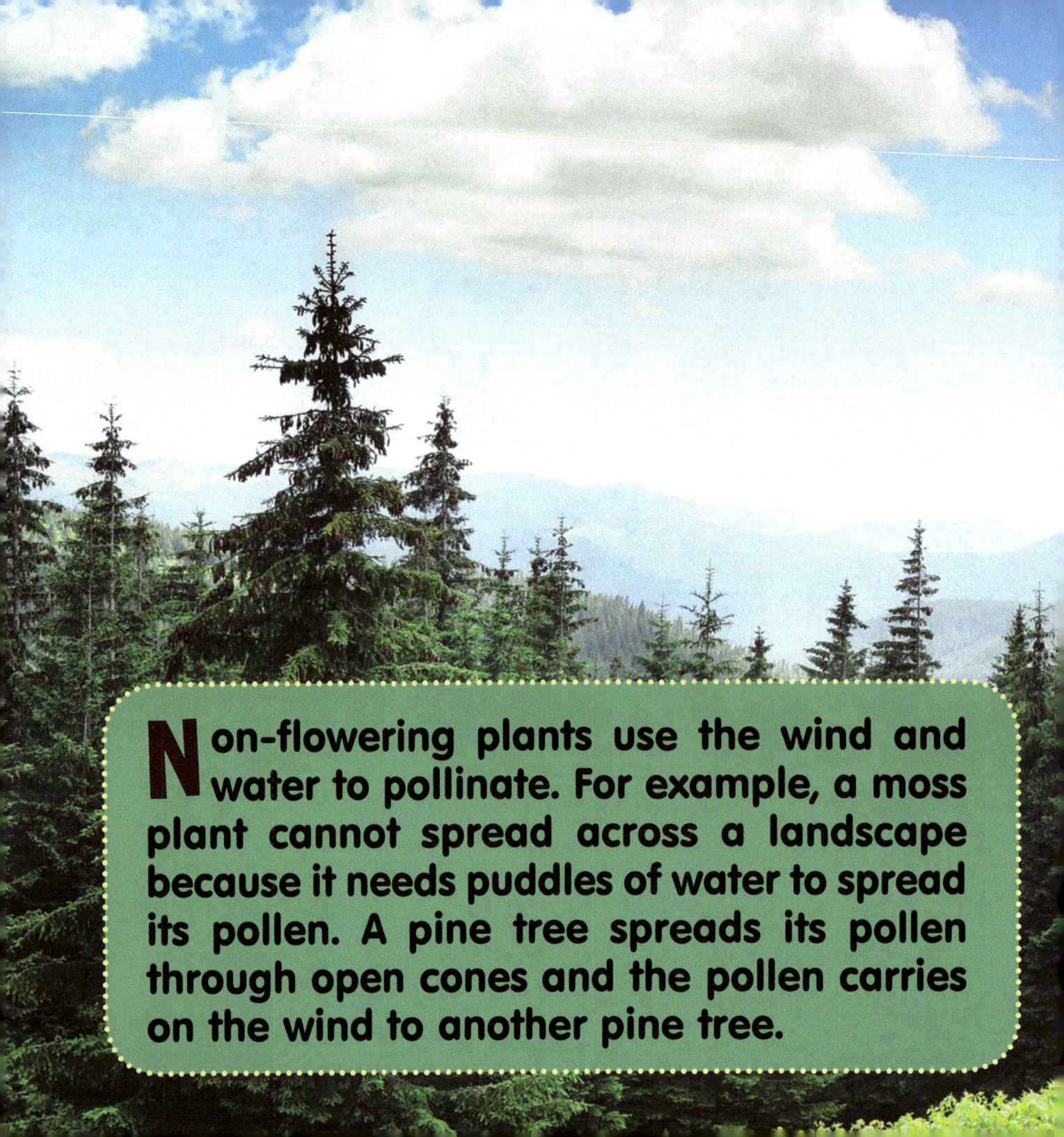

Non-flowering plants use the wind and water to pollinate. For example, a moss plant cannot spread across a landscape because it needs puddles of water to spread its pollen. A pine tree spreads its pollen through open cones and the pollen carries on the wind to another pine tree.

Although the pollen from flowering plants also spreads via wind, the help of birds, butterflies, bees, and sometimes bats helps them to have more ways to be pollinated and therefore have a better chance of successfully reproducing.

USING FLOWERING AND NON-FLOWERING PLANTS IN GARDENS

Both flowering and non-flowering plants have different kinds of beauty, so most gardeners use both in their landscape plans. Many types of non-flowering plants are evergreen, which simply means that they stay green throughout the year. Most flowering plants go through a cycle throughout the seasons.

Cultivated Plants

First, they produce green leaves during the spring and summer with flowers for birds and bees to pollinate. Then, they lose their leaves in the winter when there are less pollinators and less water around. By mixing the types of plants in a garden, gardeners can ensure that some plants will be green all year and lend some life to the garden during the winter months.

Awesome! Now you know more about both flowering and non-flowering plants. You can find more Biology Books from Baby Professor by searching the website of your favorite book retailer.

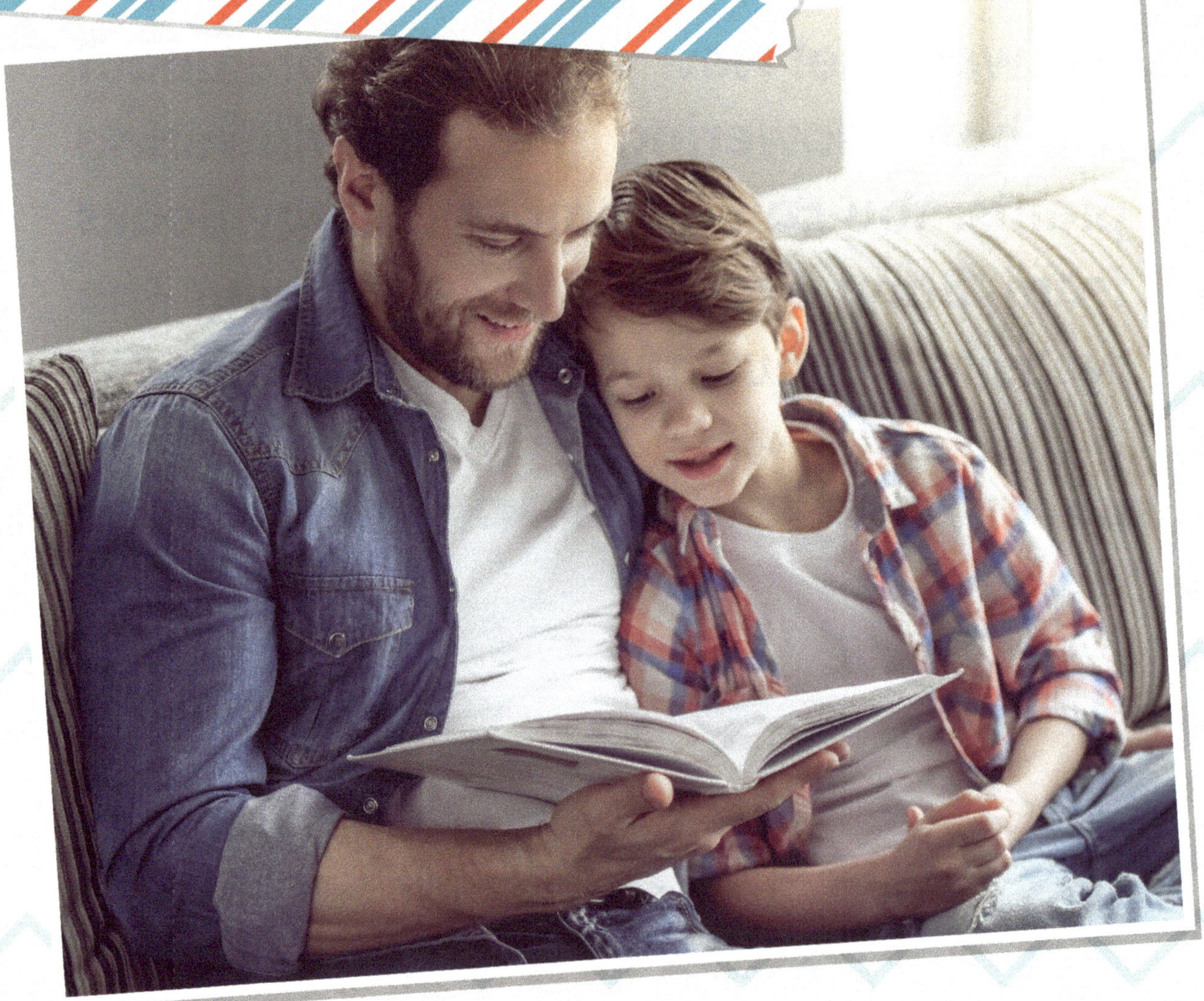

Visit

BABY PROFESSOR
EDUCATION KIDS

www.BabyProfessorBooks.com

to download Free Baby Professor eBooks and view our catalog of new and exciting Children's Books